MATTHEW

LEADER'S GUIDE
CHILDREN'S BIBLE QUIZZING MINISTRY
GAMES AND ACTIVITIES

CHILDREN'S BIBLE QUIZZING MINISTRY

SDMI
Mesoamerica Region

CHILDREN'S MINISTRIES
CHURCH OF THE NAZARENE
KIDS FIRST

children'squizzing

Children's Bible Quizzing – Games and Activities

Published by: Mesoamerica Region Discipleship Ministries

www.discipleship.MesoamericaRegion.org

www.SdmiResources.mesoamericaregion.org

ISBN: 978-1-63580-083-8

All of the scripture verses quoted are from the NIV Bible unless otherwise stated.

Adapted and Translated into English from Spanish by:
Pamela Vargas Castillo, with love for all the children of the Church of the Nazarene

Printed in the United States

TABLE OF CONTENTS

GENERAL INFORMATION

WHAT IS CHILDREN'S BIBLE QUIZZING MINISTRY (CBQM)?

This ministry is part of an effective strategy for the discipleship of children in the local church. The vision of CBQM is directed towards preparing our children to live their lives as disciples of Jesus, basing all their learning on the Word of God.

We firmly believe that instructing the "children on the way they should go" (Proverbs 22:6) is a pressing mandate that the Lord has given us, especially in our confused societies in which our children are dying - literally and spiritually. We trust that by participating in this experiential teaching of CBQM, the children will not leave the "way they should go," even when they leave their childhood behind.

The dynamic and attractive approach presented by this ministry has helped children and other participants treasure with greater strength and depth the biblical content studied. The games have been used for competition between teams based on specific topics and studies. Due to our experience over several years, we have been able to observe how the members of these teams have grown in stature, knowledge and wisdom. That is why we encourage you to learn more about this ministry and create a CBQM in your church.

WHAT RESOURCES ARE AVAILABLE FOR CBQM?

You are holding in your hand 1 of 2 books used for Children's Bible Quizzing Ministries. This book contains games and activities that will make learning God's Word so much fun. This book should be used alongside its companion book, Matthew: Leader's Guide - Lessons and Questions. That book contains 20 Bible Studies for Children over the book of Matthew, as well as Bible Quizzing Questions that can be used in traditional Children's Bible Quizzes.

WHAT IS THE PURPOSE OF CBQM?

The purpose of CBQM is to help children study the Bible in an integral and attractive way, orienting them towards practical application in their daily life. As an essential part of their discipleship starting from childhood, they are helped to develop a desire to study the Bible and learn from it. In addition, this prepares them for a ministry within the local church. CBQM provides a great environment for each child to discover in the Bible that God prepares him or her for His service, and at the same time motivates them to work as a team.

CAN I ORGANIZE A CBQM TEAM IN MY LOCAL CHURCH?

Of course. First you need to organize the CBQM. Check with your district SDMI leadership to find out if they have any organized competitions scheduled, how you can get involved, etc. If your district doesn't have events organized, talk with other local churches to start some competitions.

Each year, a different book of the Bible is studied throughout the 6 year cycle:

Annual Study Schedule

- MATTHEW - 2018
- ACTS - 2019
- GENESIS - 2020
- EXODUS - 2021
- JOSHUA, JUDGES, AND RUTH - 2022
- 1 & 2 SAMUEL – 2023
- MATTHEW - 2024

You can find more information and digital copies of the books at www.SdmiResources.mesoamericaregion.org or communicate with your area, district and/or regional leaders.

HOW DO I PREPARE THE CHILDREN FOR CBQM?

The Bible version that will be used for the memorization of verses, readings and specific words is the New International Version (NIV). To explain the teaching and go deeper into the study, one can (and must) refer to other versions of the Bible and commentaries. A teaching and study time must be established with the team. The study must focus on the book of the Bible assigned for that specific year.

To study the book of the Bible better, it can be divided into chapters or specific events. We have prepared Questions that are located at the end of the book that will guide you through this process. Start by reading about the main events, and discuss with them by asking questions about situations, characters, places and names.

Discuss information that creates curiosity in the team, such as customs, the meanings of objects or rites, and other interesting features that complement and clarify the text and context of the section being studied. Create lists of words, names, places, objects, animals. Find out in which other books of the Bible the main characters are mentioned. Have the children memorize the main texts exactly. Help them memorize events and story sequences in a non-textual way. In this way, they can relate it as completely as possible. It is necessary to help them remember important data. Guide them to discover individually and as a team the teaching of God for their lives.

THIS STUDY GUIDE CAN HELP WITH THE FOLLOWING TOPICS:
- Where does this character(s) come from?
- Who is he/she related to?
- Where does the story unfold?
- How does God work in their lives?
- Why is this story in the Bible?
- How does this passage relate to Christ, and therefore to salvation?
- Bring each story into the current time. What would it be like if it took place today?
- What values are found in the story?
- What places are mentioned? Mark them on a map.
- What are the characters like?
- What characteristics do they have?
- What things stand out in the culture, and what do you need to investigate (animals, crafts, rites or customs, etc.)?

IN ADDITION:

Invite Sunday School teachers and / or people with theological training to give lessons on specific subjects and clarify questions.

Encourage the people of the church to support the team in the composition of the lyrics and music of the song, poem, badge and in the rehearsals.

Practice for each competition only after having studied and clarified the subject well. Remember that it is important to develop the skills in which the child does best.

CATEGORIES

CBQM is divided into five categories, as detailed below:

1. Memorization Category: the purpose of this category is to help the child memorize the Bible in a dynamic and exciting way.

During a district, area, or regional competition, etc., three memorization games will be played; Children will find out the specific games only on the day of the competition.

2. Reflection Category: The objective of this category is to motivate the child to reflectively read the Bible, in terms of the spiritual teachings it contains and the context (historical, cultural, idiomatic, etc.) in which it unfolds. During a competition, two reflection games will be played. Children will find out the specific games only on the day of the competition.

3. Category of manual art: In this category, the objective is to develop in the child the skills with which they can represent the biblical knowledge learned through the handicraft. During a competition, a manual art game will be played. The children will find out which game only on the day of the competition.

4. Action category: In this category, the objective is to develop in the child the ability to express with his body a spiritual message that involves the study of the Word of God. During a competition, an action game will be played. The children will know the game only on the day of the competition.

5. Music category: In this category, the goal is for the child to praise God through music and singing with knowledge and understanding. During a competition, a music game will be played. The children will know the game only on the day of the competition.

IN ADDITION:
Each team must have:

A name for their team, which should be based on the theme of the study and must be presented in a creative way. This will have a value of 10 points.

A badge that identifies their team. This can be a shirt, a hat, a uniform, etc. The presentation of your badge, and the badge itself, will have a value of 10 points.

A mascot, which preferably should be an animal that is related to the theme of the study and that is contained in a biblical teaching. The costume must be creative, and the presentation of the mascot has a value of 20 points.

A team cheer. This should be based on the subject of study and the name of the team, must not contain words or offensive ideas to other teams, its maximum duration is 1 minute, and its creative presentation will have a value of 20 points.

GOSPEL OF MATTHEW

BRIEF INTRODUCTION

The Gospel bears the name of Matthew - a tax collector who left his job to follow Jesus (9:9) It was written around 80 A.D. and is aimed primarily at Christians of Jewish origin.

Given the character of the addressees, Matthew often cites verses from the Old Testament and relies on them to show that God's plan, announced by the Prophets, reached its complete fulfillment in the person and work of Jesus. He is the "Son of David," the one sent to save his People, the "Son of man" who will manifest himself as the universal Judge, the "King of Israel" and the "Son of God" par excellence. Matthew also explicitly applies to Jesus the oracles of Isaiah about the "Suffering Servant" who carries our weaknesses and infirmities. And by giving him the title of "Lord," reserved only for God in the Old Testament, he implicitly affirms his divinity.

This evangelist attributes a special importance to Jesus' teachings, and groups them into five discourses, which form the plot of his Gospel, and are framed by numerous narrative sections. The central theme of these discourses is "The Kingdom of God." In them, Christ appears as "the new Moses," which brings to completion the Law of the Old Covenant. He is also the "Teacher" who teaches "as one who has authority" (7:29), the "justice" of that Kingdom inaugurated and proclaimed by him.

The Gospel of Matthew has rightly been called "the Gospel of the Church" because of the important role occupied in it by the life and organization of the community gathered in the name of Jesus. This community is the new "People of God," the place where the risen Lord manifests his presence and radiates it to all men. That is why they church is called to live in brotherly love and mutual service as indispensable conditions in making the true face of Jesus Christ visible to the world.

"And he said: 'Truly I tell you, unless you change and become like little children, you will never enter the kingdom of heaven.'" (Matthew 18:3)

MEMORIZATION CATEGORY

TELL ME THE ANSWER

SCORE	TIME	PARTICIPANTS	MODE
20 points per correct answer	1 minute	2 per team	One team at a time

The questions consist of a series of characteristics that describe a biblical theme or character. The characteristics are in order and related to each other. The moderator must have two questions for each participating team. Each participant must answer their question without consulting with his/her teammate. The participant has one minute to give the answer. If the answer is correct, the moderator says "**CORRECT**" and the judges award 20 points to the team (for each correct answer). If the answer is not correct or is not answered in the given time, the participant loses their chance and the moderator gives the correct answer. (No points are awarded to the team.) The moderator continues with a participant from the other team, that is, the moderator alternates between the teams, with one answering at a time.

FOUL: If a judge observes that a participant consults with his/her team or someone else present, the moderator will cancel the question and ask a different question. If the participant has already been caught doing this before, the moderator will cancel the question and the team loses its opportunity.

EXAMPLES:

I am engaged to Joseph and I am the mother of Jesus. Who I am? **ANSWER / Mary (Matthew 1:18)**	We saw the star of the king of the Jews in the east, and we were worshiping him. Who are we? **A / Magi (Matthew 2:1-2)**	We are the presents that the Magi took when they went to see Jesus What are we? **A / gold, frankincense and myrrh (Matthew 2:11)**
We are brothers and we are fishermen. We are also the sons of Zebedee. Who are we? **A / James and John (Matthew 4:21)**	I sit in the bank of public taxes and collect taxes. Who I am? **A / Matthew (Matthew 9:9)**	With very little, a great miracle was done, God worked and the crowd was nourished. What are we? **A / Five loaves and two fishes (Matthew 14:17)**
Jesus asked us, "Who do you say that I am?" I answered, "You are the Christ, the Son of the living God." Who I am? **A / Simon Peter (Matthew 16:16)**	We seek Jesus to tempt him, accuse him and point him out. Who are we? **A / The Pharisees (Matthew 19:3)**	I wrapped the body of Jesus in a clean sheet and put it in a new tomb. Who am I? **A / Joseph from Arimathea (Matthew 27:57-60)**

PUZZLE

SCORE	TIME	PARTICIPANTS	MODE
30 points	The one that finishes first	3 per team	Simultaneous

Use the same verse for both teams. select the verse from the suggested list for memorization at the end of this guide. The verse must be divided into 9 pieces.

Items needed: a spoon (serving or soup) for each participant and one lemon or ball per team.

This competition consists of putting the pieces of the puzzle together on the floor. When completed, it should form one of the Bible verses that the children have memorized.

Participants are situated one behind the other in their teams three meters away from the puzzle. The first participant takes a spoon and puts it in his mouth, and then puts the lemon or ball on the spoon in his mouth. The participant then goes to the puzzle, places the spoon and the lemon/ball to one side, and then arranges one piece of the puzzle in horizontal form. He then takes the spoon and the lemon/ball and goes back to the next participant on his team and hands him the lemon/ball by passing it with his spoon onto his teammate's spoon. They repeat the same action and so on until the puzzle is finished. (If the child drops the spoon or lemon, he must return to the starting point and start again.

Consultation is allowed, only among the 3 participants.

Participating teams begin at the same time. The team that finishes first with the correct answer is the winner and receives 30 points. If there is a tie between teams, the 30 points are awarded to each team.

FOUL: If a judge observes one of the children holding the lemon/ball or spoon with their hand, or if they throw the spoon or lemon and continue without returning to their place of departure, the judge will inform the moderator, and the child must return to the place of departure to restart the journey.

If one of the participants places more than one piece of the puzzle, the judge will indicate that to the moderator, and the moderator will remove one of the pieces of the puzzle and return it to the pile of pieces.

From that time	**on Jesus**	**began to preach**
"Repent,	**for the kingdom**	**of heaven**
has come	**near"**	**Matthew 4:17**

CROSSWORD

SCORE	TIME	PARTICIPANTS	MODE
10 points per correct answer	5 minutes	3 per team	Simultaneous

Items needed:

- A copy of the same crossword puzzle for each participating team
- One pencil per team.

Each team is given a crossword puzzle of 6 or 8 questions. Each team is given five minutes to answer. Teams must submit their crossword puzzle in the allotted time. At the end of the five minutes, 10 points are awarded for each correct answer. Consultation is only allowed among the 3 participants of the team.

FOUL: If team members consult with the coach or other children of the team who are not participating, the judge will inform the moderator and the moderator will disqualify the crossword of that team, thereby eliminating their participation in this game only.

EXAMPLE: Based on Matthew, chapter 4

Horizontal:

1. How many days and nights did Jesus fast? Answer / Forty
2. To what part of the temple did the devil take Jesus? A / Pinnacle (highest point of the temple)
3. Where did Peter and Andrew throw their net? A / Sea
4. Who came when the devil left him? A / Angels

Vertical:

5. What did James and John mend? A / Nets
6. What did the tempter tell Jesus to turn the stones into? R /Bread
7. What did Peter and Andrew do for a living? A / Fishermen
8. Where did Jesus return to when he heard that John was in prison? A / Galilee

COMPLETE THE WORD

SCORE	TIME	PARTICIPANTS	MODE
10 points	5 seconds per answer	**1 per team**	One team at a time

Items needed: a slate or large sheet of bond paper, a marker or chalk, a picture divided into 5 pieces to assemble, a list of words with the same number of letters (minimum of 6 letters and a maximum of 12), one word per participating team and some additional.

This game is based on the game "hangman" or "Wheel of Fortune." Provide as many spaces as there are letters in the word the participant has to discover. A sub-theme related to the word is specified. For example: Places, friendships, teachings, writings, family, objects, characteristics, etc.

The participant must say letters to complete the word. She/he has 5 seconds to give a letter. If she exceeds the time without saying a letter, that is considered an error. If she says a letter that is part of the word, it is placed in the blank space(s) as many times as it appears in the word. If the letter mentioned is not part of the word, it is considered an error and the letter is written to the side in view of the participant as an aid not to repeat it.

If, when filling in the blank spaces of the word, she discovers the hidden word, she can say it, and she has successful completed the game. If it is not correct, it is considered an error. The participant can make a maximum of 5 errors. These errors are visualized with the picture that has been divided up into 5 pieces. Each time an error is made, another piece of the picture is added. If the participant does not discover the word before 5 errors are made, the picture is completed and the moderator says the word. The team does not get any points.

If the participant discovers the correct word before completing the picture, their team receives 10 points. If he doesn't discover the word, his team does not receive any point.

Then it is the next team's turn.

FOUL: If the participant consults with another team member or anyone else, the judge will inform the moderator, and the moderator will cancel the word to complete, and start again with another word if this is the first offense. If the infraction is repeated, the participant is disqualified and the team is no longer eligible to compete in this particular game.

Example of picture divided into parts:

Example: Topic is "Character"

The participant starts with 8 blank spaces.   __ __ __ __ __ __ __ __

He must guess a letter. If he guesses an "M", the moderator or helper would then write an "M" in each of the appropriate spaces on the board or large paper for all to see.

___ M̲ M̲ __ __ __ __ __

The participant then guesses another letter. If he guesses an "R", this is incorrect. The moderator or helper would write an "R" to the side so the participant can see that they have already chosen that letter so they won't guess it again. Also, one part of the picture will be placed on the board/paper.

The participant guesses another letter. If he guess an "E", that letter would be added in the appropriate blank space. ___ M̲ M̲ __ __ __ E̲ __

If the participant next guesses a "T", this is an error. The letter is written to the side and another piece is added to the picture.

The game continues until the participant completes or correctly discovers the word (10 points for the team), or the picture is completed after 5 errors (game over – 0 points for the team).

Then it is the next team's turn.

Examples of Topics and Words:

Topic: Characters								
1	2	3	4	5	6	7	8	Ref.
I	M	M	A	N	U	E	L	1:23
N	E	P	H	T	A	L	I	4:15
M	A	T	T	H	E	W		9:9
Z	E	B	U	L	U	N		4:15
Z	E	B	E	D	E	E		4:21

Topic: Places									
1	2	3	4	5	6	7	8	9	Ref.
N	A	Z	A	R	E	T	H		2:23
G	A	L	I	L	E	E			2:22
B	E	T	H	P	H	A	G	E	21:1
J	E	R	U	S	A	L	E	M	23:37
B	E	T	H	A	N	Y			21:17
G	O	L	G	O	T	H	A		27:33

Topic: Objects									
1	2	3	4	5	6	7	8	9	Ref.
T	R	E	A	S	U	R	E	S	2:11
T	H	O	R	N	S				13:7
M	U	S	T	A	R	D			13:31
B	A	S	K	E	T	S			13:48

Topic: Animals							
1	2	3	4	5	6	7	Ref.
L	O	C	U	S	T	S	3:4
C	A	M	E	L	S		3:4
V	I	P	E	R	S		3:7
S	H	E	E	P			10:16
W	O	L	V	E	S		10:16
D	O	N	K	E	Y		21:2

ALPHABET SOUP

SCORE	TIME	PARTICIPANTS	MODE
5 points per correct answer	7 minutes	2 per team	Simultaneous team competition

Items needed: Word-search puzzles with ten words to discover – sufficient number for each participating team to receive one copy. The moderator must prepare a least 2 different puzzles in case of fouls.

Each team will receive the same puzzle at the same time.

Each team must discover the words that appear horizontally, vertically, diagonally, top to bottom, left to right or vice versa. Consultation on the puzzle will only be between the two participants of the team.

When a team finishes, they must take their completed puzzle to one of the judges for review (the time is recorded). (The other teams continue working on their puzzles.) If the judge observes that the team has found all of the correct words, he/she will inform the moderator. The competition stops and one of the participants reads the list aloud and that team wins 40 points. If the word puzzle is incorrect on some word(s), the judge will simply say "Incorrect" and the team will continue to search for words.

Maximum time for this competition is 7 minutes. If no team finishes during the set time, the competition is scored according to the correct answers (5 points per correct answer).

FOUL: If a participant consults with anyone besides their participating team partner, the judge will inform the moderator and the team's puzzle will be changed to different one and they must start over again. The team will be disqualified on the second Foul.

EXAMPLE: Based on Matthew 10:1-4

T	H	O	M	A	S	T	J	S	E	V	J
W	W	E	R	T	J	B	A	O	G	T	U
S	E	W	D	R	G	N	M	A	H	Q	D
C	M	E	F	P	E	T	E	R	C	N	A
S	O	H	G	A	T	D	S	D	R	T	S
A	L	T	N	S	F	C	N	I	B	N	O
Q	O	T	O	F	X	I	C	A	M	P	L
T	H	A	D	D	A	E	U	S	H	O	A
Y	T	M	S	D	F	G	B	N	B	C	N
H	R	F	G	R	G	W	E	R	D	N	A
J	A	A	S	E	R	M	K	O	G	V	P
K	B	S	P	H	I	L	I	P	C	P	E

T	H	O	M	A	S	T	J	S	E	V	J
W	W	E	R	T	J	B	A	O	G	T	U
S	E	W	D	R	G	N	M	A	H	Q	D
C	M	E	F	P	E	T	E	R	C	N	A
S	O	H	G	A	T	D	S	D	R	T	S
A	L	T	N	S	F	C	N	I	B	N	O
Q	O	T	O	F	X	I	C	A	M	P	L
T	H	A	D	D	A	E	U	S	H	O	A
Y	T	M	S	D	F	G	B	N	B	C	N
H	R	F	G	R	G	W	E	R	D	N	A
J	A	A	S	E	R	M	K	O	G	V	P
K	B	S	P	H	I	L	I	P	C	P	E

MAGIC WORD

SCORE	TIME	PARTICIPANTS	MODE
10 points	1 minute	1 per team	Simultaneous

Items needed: Two different word puzzles should be prepared for each team participating, a marker or chalk for each team.

The word puzzles are placed on the wall, blackboard or table and the game is started immediately. No team may see the puzzle before the competition is started. The game is played simultaneously by all participating teams. Each team will work on a different puzzle. The search starts from the letter with the star, and the participants must draw a line in any direction, even diagonally, to join the letters and find the word. The letter must be adjacent horizontally, vertically, or diagonally to connect. When a participant finds the word, he must write it on the line below the puzzle and have a judge verify it.

Maximum time: one minute to discover the word. The first participant to correctly discover and connect the letters for the word wins. If there is a tie, 10 points is awarded to each team. If a participant incorrectly does their puzzle, the referee who checks it indicates that it is incorrect and the team is immediately disqualified and the game continues with the rest of the participants. If none of the teams manage to discover the word, no team receives points.

NOTE: The judge must record the time that each puzzle is completed in case there is a disagreement of who finished first.

FOUL: If anyone present says the word aloud, the judge will indicate it. This game is void, and no team gets points. The game is restarted with a new word game for each team.

Examples:

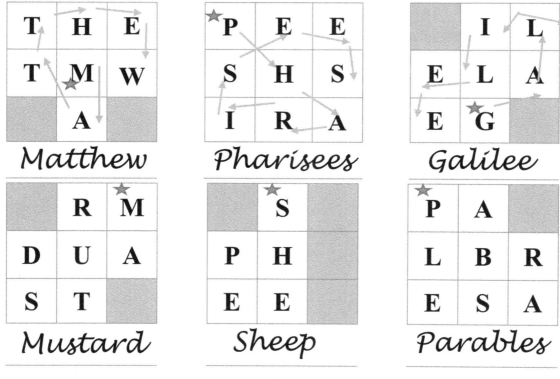

Matthew   Pharisees   Galilee

Mustard   Sheep   Parables

BIBLE GEOGRAPHY

SCORE	TIME	PARTICIPANTS	MODE
5 points per correct name	Complete Bible Reading	3 per team	Simultaneous

Items needed: For this game, a map of the area studied is required, maximum letter size (8.5 x 11 inches), a marker or pen and 2 Bible passages previously prepared or indicated in the Bible.

Each team is provided with a map. The Bible passage is read and the team should mark the places mentioned in the reading. The reading is not repeated, nor are questions or interruptions accepted. Participants on the same team can consult each other in a low voice. At the end of the reading, the judges review the maps. 5 points are awarded for each map location correctly marked.

FOUL: The interruption of the reading with questions or requests, getting out of your place, consulting with each other in loud voices, or consulting with anyone other than the 3 participants is considered a foul. If a foul occurs, the judge will inform the moderator to draw attention to the problem at once. If it is repeated on a second occasion, the game is paused and the team is disqualified from the game. Then the rest of the participating teams will continue with the game.

EXAMPLE: Based on Matthew 21:1-17

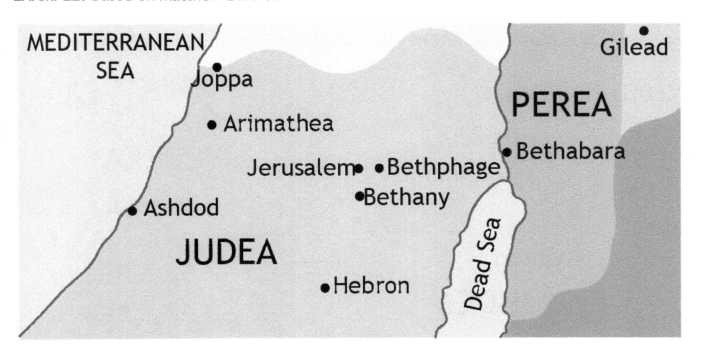

BIBLICAL GEOGRAPHY, BASED ON MATTHEW 21: 1-17

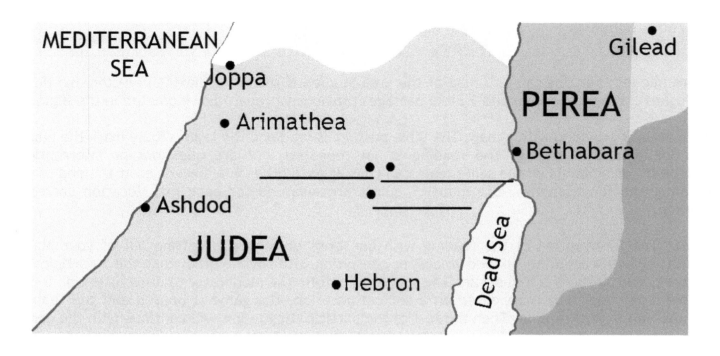

BIBLICAL GEOGRAPHY, BASED ON MATTHEW 21: 1-17

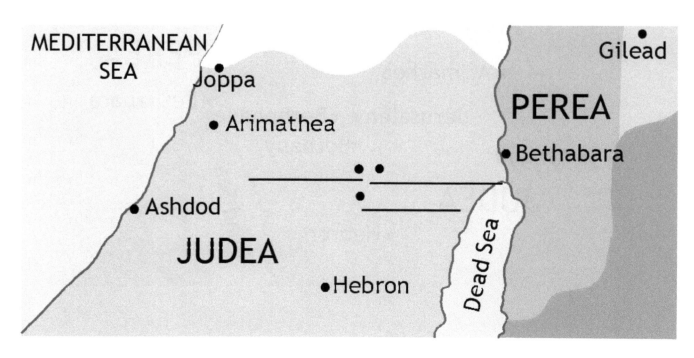

COMPLETE THE STORY

SCORE	TIME	PARTICIPANTS	MODE
30 points	1 minute	3 per team	One team at a time

The moderator will have a list of biblical passages to read, one for each participating team. The biblical passages must be different, but they must have the same number of verses. The moderator begins by reading the biblical passage to one team. As soon as one of the three participants of the team recognizes what passage it refers to, he or she must interrupt the moderator by rising from his/her place to continue the story. The time begins the moment the moderator starts reading and stops when the participant gets up. The judges record this time. The moderator instructs the participant to finish the story. The participant has 1 minute to do so. When the participant finishes the story, the moderator announces if the rest of the story is correct or not, and the time obtained. If the story is not correct, the moderator announces "INCORRECT." If 2 or 3 participants of the team get up at the same time, they must immediately decide which participant will continue.

The moderator then repeats the process with another passage for the next team.

NOTE: The winning team is the one who correctly finishes the story and has the shortest time elapsed during the reading of the moderator. Consultation between the 3 participants of the team is allowed, but only quietly. The time judge must make sure that the participant does not exceed the 1 minute time limit to complete the story.

If one of the participants gets up from his place to finish the story, but forgets the rest of the story, he is given 15 seconds to start his response. If he remains silent or sits down again, the judge indicates "INCORRECT" to the moderator, ending the participation of that team in this competition.

Examples of story passages that could be used:

- **The Sermon on the Mount (5:1-12)**

- **Jesus Sends Out the Twelve (10:1-15)**

- **The Parable of the Sower (13:1-13)**

- **Jesus Comes to Jerusalem as King (21:1-11)**

- **The Parable of the Bags of Gold (25:14-30)**

- **The Crucifixion of Jesus (25:32-50)**

- **Jesus Has Risen (28:1-10)**

THE KEY LETTER

SCORE	TIME	PARTICIPANTS	MODE
30 points	1 minute	3 per team	Simultaneous

Items needed: white/chalk board or large pieces of paper for each participating team, markers or chalk for each team, 2 envelopes with category and letter for each participating team (1 extra in case of foul).

The moderator will give a sealed envelope that will contain a category (characters, places, objects, animals, miscellaneous) and a base letter to each participating team. The teams will participate simultaneously by writing a list of words related to the selected category containing the specific base letter they received in their envelope. The 3 participants will form a line three meters away from the board. When the moderator gives the signal, the first participant of each team goes to the board and writes a qualifying word, then returns to their team and hands the marker/chalk to the next participant of his team. That second participant then goes to the board and writes the second word and so on until the time limit of one minute is over.

The winning team will be the team with the most correct words after 1 minute.

NOTE: The participant can run or walk to and from the board.

FOUL: If the judge observes that teammates are speaking among themselves after the competition has begun, or someone from the audience says a word in a loud voice, the judge will tell the moderator and the game will stop, and then start again with a different category and letter for each team. If it happens a second time, the team will be disqualified from the game, or the person from the audience will be asked to leave the competition room.

Topic: People - Letter A

		A						
	M	A	T	T	H	E	W	/
	M	A	R	Y				/
		A	N	D	R	E	W	/
J	U	D	A	S				/
	J	A	M	E	S			X

Topic: Places - Letter E

				E							
			B	E	T	A	N	Y			/
G	A	L	I	L	E	E					/
				E	G	Y	P	T			/
		J	U	D	E	A					/
J	E	R	U	S	A	L	E	M			X

Topic: Animals - Letter I

		I					
	F	I	S	H			/
	V	I	P	E	R	S	/
	P	I	G	S			/
C	H	I	C	K	E	N	/
	C	A	M	E	L		X

Topic: Objects - Letter O

			O						
		G	O	L	D				/
		L	O	A	V	E	S		/
	C	L	O	T	H	E	S		/
	S	T	O	N	E	S			/
	C	R	O	W	D	S			/

MEMORY

SCORE	TIME	PARTICIPANTS	MODE
10 points for each correct answer	5 minutes	2 per team	Simultaneously

The moderator will prepare 16 cards with memory verses. The verses will go on 8 cards and the biblical citations on the other 8 cards. The teams will have 5 minutes to connect the pairs on the floor or table. If more than one team correctly connects all 8 pairs, the team that does it first will be awarded 10 bonus points. The judge will also give 10 points to each team for each of their correct pairs.

EXAMPLE:

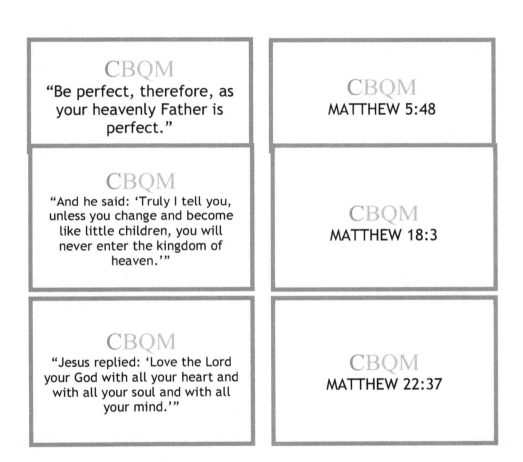

NOTE: You can find the complete list of memory verses at the end of this book.

STOP

SCORE	TIME	PARTICIPANTS	MODE
60 points	2 minutes	1 per team	Simultaneous

Items needed: 1 answer sheet and a pen/pencil for each team.

The moderator will give 1 answer sheet to each team with the following titles: LETTER; NAME OF PERSON; OBJECT, ANIMAL or PLANT; PLACE; and TOTAL. (See example below.) The moderator starts the game by beginning to recite the alphabet in a loud voice, starting with the letter "A" and continues the alphabet in a low voice. A judge will say STOP! at a certain point, and the game with start with the letter that the moderator was saying when the judge said STOP! The moderator will say the first letter to be used for the game , and then begins the count of 2 minutes for the participants to answer.

The child who finishes his/her answer sheet first must say out loud, "STOP!" Then the other participants will no longer be able to fill in more answers. Next, a second letter will be chosen, and the 2nd round begins. After playing the two suggested rounds, the children hand in their answer sheets. If there are correct words that are repeated on the answer sheets of other participants, those answers receive 5 points each. For the answers that are correct and not repeated, they receive 10 points each.

NOTE: It is suggested that the game last for two rounds (letters).

FOUL: If the judge sees that a participant continues writing down answers after another participant has said STOP!, that participant's answer sheet is disqualified.

EXAMPLE:

Name:							
LETTER	**NAME OF PERSON**	**points**	**OBJECT, ANIMAL OR PLANT**	**points**	**PLACE**	**points**	**TOTAL**
						FINAL SCORE	

Name: Team:

Name: Mary Cole					Team: Jesus Disciples		
LETTER	**NAME OF PERSON**	**points**	**OBJECT, ANIMAL OR PLANT**	**points**	**PLACE**	**points**	**TOTAL**
T	Thaddaeus	10	Tree	10	Tyre	10	30
M	Mary	5	Mustard	10	Magadan	10	25
						FINAL SCORE	55

Name: Alex Sykes					Team: In the boat with Jesus		
LETTER	**NAME OF PERSON**	**points**	**OBJECT, AMINAL OR PLANT**	**points**	**PLACE**	**points**	**TOTAL**
T	Thomas	10	Teeth	10		0	20
M	Mary	5	Mountain	10		0	15
						FINAL SCORE	35

BIBLE DETECTIVE

SCORE	TIME	PARTICIPANTS	MODE
20 points	-------	2 per team	One team at a time

The moderator will prepare a sealed envelope with a Bible character's name inside, and a participation number on the outside, for each team that will participate in the game. Each team will take an envelope, and participate according to their number, with number 1 starting. Each team will have a detective (give that person a magnifying glass of any material to signify being a detective), and an answer-giver. When it is their team's turn, the answer-giver will open their envelope and see the name of their biblical character. He/she must not reveal the name to the detective.

Then the detective may ask the answer-giver 5 questions in order to discover the name of their Bible character. The answer-giver can only respond to the questions with answers of "Yes," "NO," or a one word answer. If the detective correctly guesses the Biblical character within 5 questions, the team receives 20 points. If he does not discover the biblical character, the team will not receive any points, and the moderator will announce the correct answer out loud.

Examples:

Character:

MATTHEW

Possible Questions that the detective could ask their answer-giver, and the answer-giver's answers are in parentheses:

1. Is it a man or a woman? (Man)
2. Was he a disciple of Jesus? (Yes)
3. Did he have a mother-in-law? (No)
4. Was he a fisherman? (No)
5. What letter does his name begin with? (M)

Character:

PETER

Possible Questions and answers:

1. Is it a man or a woman? (Man)
2. Was he one of Jesus' disciples? (Yes)
3. Did he have a brother? (Yes)
4. Was he a fisherman? (Yes)
5. Was James his brother? (No)

TWO-EDGED SWORD

SCORE	TIME	PARTICIPANTS	MODE
10 points for each correct answer	1 minute per question	1 per team	One team at a time

The moderator must prepare a questionnaire with three different questions for each participant, and put them in envelopes with participation numbers on the outside. Each participants will take an envelope, and number 1 starts. He/she will give the envelope to the moderator who will then ask the first of three True/False questions for the participant to answer. The participant has one minute to answer the question once the question is asked. And then the next question is asked.

NOTE: If the participant does not answer in the given time, or answers incorrectly, the moderator will announce the correct answer out loud, and the judge will not award any points for that question.

EXAMPLE:

ENVELOPE 1:
  1. Abraham's son was named Isaac.
     TRUE OR FALSE   ANSWER/ TRUE (1:2)

  1. John the Baptist dressed in sheep's hair clothes with a belt of locusts.
     TRUE OR FALSE   A/ FALSE (3:4)

  2. Simon Peter and his brother Andrew were sons of Zebedee.
     TRUE OR FALSE   A/ FALSE (4: 18-21)

ENVELOPE 2:
  1. "These people honor me with their lips, but their heart is far from me" was a prophecy of Isaiah.
     TRUE OR FALSE   A / TRUE (15:8)

  2. The disciples were the ones who asked Jesus, "Who is the greatest in the kingdom of heaven?"
     TRUE OR FALSE   A / TRUE (18:1)

  3. Judas was given forty pieces of silver for betraying Jesus.
     TRUE OR FALSE   A / FALSE (26:15)

THE DICE

SCORE	TIME	PARTICIPANTS	MODE
20 points	30 seconds	1 per team	One team at a time

The moderator prepares a die on which actions will be written on each side: SING A SONG, SAY A VERSE, CHARACTERISTICS OF A BIBLE CHARACTER. Each team draws a participation number. The moderator starts with number 1. Number 1 participant is called forward, rolls the die, and then has 30 seconds to do the activity that comes up on the top of the die. If the participant is able to do the action, the judge gives 20 points to the team. If the participant doesn't do the action or remains silent during the 30 seconds, the judge will not award a score. Next, the moderator will call up the next participant to roll the die, and so forth until each team has participated.

EXAMPLE:

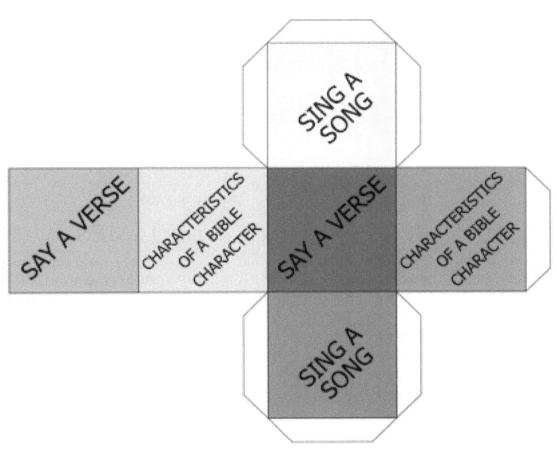

Example: Characteristics of a Bible character

PETER
Peter was a fisherman who had a brother named Andrew. Jesus found them on the Sea of Galilee and called them to be his disciples. Peter had a mother-in-law who was very sick with a fever and Jesus healed her. Peter wanted to walk on the water like Jesus. He also believed that Jesus was the Christ, the son of the living God. Peter had difficulties in forgiving and staying awake. Peter denied Jesus three times.

CONNECT (NEW GAME)

SCORE	TIME	PARTICIPANTS	MODE
20 points	2 minutes	2 per team	Simultaneous

The moderator must prepare an envelope with three pairs of characters for each team; each pair of characters must be related or connected to each other in some way, for example: BROTHERS, FRIENDS, BOTH WERE AT AN EVENT, etc. Each envelope must contain the same characters.

The envelope is given to each team and they are given a start signal. From the start signal, each team has 2 minutes to match their characters into 3 pairs. When a team has 3 pairs, they must yell "CONNECTED!" The other teams continue matching their pairs until time is called. The first team to finish must explain to the judges what relationship their pairs have, i.e., why they matched them up. If they have good reasons why they connected each of their pairs, their team receives 20 points, and the game is over. However, if one or more pairs is not correct, no points are scored for that team and the second team to finish within the 2 minutes is given a turn to explain their pairs, and so on.

NOTE: In case two teams say CONNECTED! at the same time, both must give their explanations and if they are correct, 20 points is given for both teams.

MATTHEW   JESUS

Matthew was a tax collector whom Jesus called to follow him and be his disciple.

PETER   ANDREW

They were both fishermen, brothers and used to fish in the Sea of Galilee, where Jesus found them and called them to be his disciples.

JAMES   JOHN

They were both fishermen, brothers, sons of Zebedee, and Jesus called them to be his disciples.

Other pairs:
Mary Magdalene and the other Mary (27:61, 28:1);
Pilate and Barabbas (27:17);
Jesus and John the Baptist (3:13-14) Jesus and the woman with the alabaster jar (26: 7)

FISHERMEN (NEW GAME)

SCORE	TIME	PARTICIPANTS	MODE
10 points	1 minute	1 per team	One team at a time

Several cards are prepared in the form of fish, and a statement is written on one side having to do with a Bible passage which mentions FISH, FISHING, FISHERMEN, NETS. The participants line up. The first participant must take a fish, read the partial statement/clue, and then has 1 minute to give his/her response, which would be a brief explanation of the event and the biblical reference where it is located. 10 points are given to the team for a correct answer. Then, the next participant picks a fish, and so forth.

FOUL: If the judge sees a participant consult with someone on his team, or someone in the audience says the answer out loud, the team is disqualified and no points are given to that team.

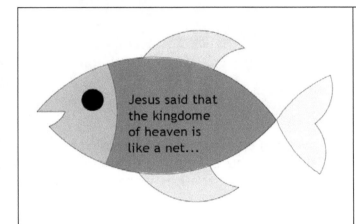

Possible answer:

"Once again, the kingdom of heaven is like a net that was let down into the lake and caught all kinds of fish. When it was full, the fishermen pulled it up on the shore. Then they sat down and collected the good fish in baskets, but threw the bad away."

MATTHEW 13:47-48

Possible answer:

"As Jesus was walking beside the Sea of Galilee, he saw two brothers, Simon called Peter and his brother Andrew. They were casting a net into the lake, for they were fishermen. 'Come, follow me,' Jesus said, 'and I will send you out to fish for people.' At once they left their nets and followed him."

MATTHEW 4:18-20

REFLECTION CATEGORY

BIBLE BINGO

SCORE	TIME	PARTICIPANTS	MODE
30 points	The time it takes to read the Bible passage.	2 per team	Simultaneous

(This is similar to the popular game BINGO, using words instead of numbers, and one must fill up the whole card, not just a row.)

The moderator prepares a ½ or ¼ page sized game card with 9 squares drawn on it for each participant (see next page for an example). Each square will have 1 word in it. All of the words will be different words taken from the scripture passage to be read by the moderator. 8 out of the 9 words will be different than all of the other words on all of the other game cards that all of the other participants have. However, the 9th word in each group will contain the same word – it will be the last word of the biblical passage. (Look at the example on the next page.) You can see that every word on every game card is different except the key word, which is the last word of the passage, which is "ME.")

Each participant will also be given 9 small objects that will be used as game pieces or markers (beans, corn, buttons, bottle caps, plastic disks, etc.)

When it is time to start, each participant will place their game card and small game pieces in front of themselves on the table, and familiarize themselves with the words on their game card. The moderator will begin to read the chosen biblical passage. (The passage must be no shorter than ten verses and cannot last for more than 3 minutes.) While the moderator reads, the participants must listen carefully to the reading. When the moderator reads a word that is written on a participant's game card, that participant will place one of their game pieces/markers on their game card. (Similar to the game BINGO.) Whoever fills her/his game card first yells out "FINISHED." The first person who finishes their game card and yells out will receive 30 points for their team.

NOTE: If there is a tie between teams, 30 points will be awarded to each team. If there is a tie between 2 participants of the same team, only 30 points are given. If at the end of the passage reading, no participant has completely filled their card, nobody gets points.

FOUL: If a team interrupts or asks questions during the reading, the judge will take away 2 points from that team.

EXAMPLE: Based on "The Resurrection" - Matthew 28:1-10 (key word: Me)

SABBATH	DEAD	RISEN
WORSHIPED	MARY MAGDALENE	JOY
ANGEL	ME	EARTHQUAKE

WORSHIPED	SNOW	CLASPED
GUARDS	TOMB	LORD
STONE	ME	LIGHTNING

CLOTHES	ME	SABBATH
GALILEE	JESUS	DEAD
ANGEL	JOY	FEET

SNOW	JOY	GUARDS
"GREETINGS"	TOMB	AFRAID
MARY MAGDALENE	ME	EARTHQUAKE

ME	GALILEE	WORSHIPED
SNOW	JESUS	TOMB
AFRAID	CRUCIFIED	CLASPED

"GREETINGS"	ME	DEAD
DISCIPLES	CRUCIFIED	AFRAID
RISEN	TOMB	JESUS

MODERN DAY BIBLE

SCORE	TIME	PARTICIPANTS	MODE
30 points	3 minutes (2 to consult the bible and discuss together, 1 to narrate)	3 per team	One team at a time

The moderator prepares sealed envelopes containing the bible references for the biblical passage to be narrated, and a participation number on the outside. This bible reference will be different for each team. Each team will choose an envelope.

When the start is called, the first team has 2 minutes to open their envelope and look up the Bible verse and discuss the passage together. After 2 minutes, the participants must close their Bible and can no longer look at it or talk among themselves about it. The 3 participants decide who will be their presenter. The presenter then has 1 minute to tell a modern-day version of the story as if it were happening today.

When Team 1 is finishes, the moderator will have team two open their envelope and so on.

Each team who successfully tells the story will receive 30 points.

FOUL: If the participants consult among themselves after the 2 minutes is finished, or with anyone else during their turn, their team will be disqualified and no points will be awarded to the team.

Examples of Bible passages that can be used:

- **Love for Enemies 5:43-48**
- **Jesus Raises a Dead Girl and Heals a Sick Woman 9:18-26**
- **The Rich and the Kingdom of God 19:16-30**
- **The Parable of the Bags of Gold 25:14-30**
- **The Great Commission 28:16-20**

CASES

SCORE	TIME	PARTICIPANTS	MODE
20 points	1 minute	1 per team	One team at a time

Items needed: A different Case study with 2 Bible references for each participant, each of the Bible Verses written out on a 8.5x11 size or larger piece of paper, tape to attach the Bible references to the wall or board.

The order of participation can be decided by participants choosing numbers, etc. The moderator will select for the first participant the first case study (story from real life), which will have 2 biblical references, one that applies to the story and the other which doesn't. The two Bible verses in their entirety should be taped to the wall or board so that the participant can see them. Then the moderator will read the case study aloud. When the story has been read, the participant must choose which text he considers appropriate for the case study, and explain the reason for his choice. The participant has 1 minute to give his answer. If the verse and explanation are correct, the judge will give 20 points to the team. If the participant chooses the correct verse, but the explanation is incorrect, he only gets 10 points. If everything is incorrect, the moderator will say the correct answer and the team will not receive any points.

Then the moderator will move on to the second team and the second case study, going through the same process.

FOUL: If someone in the audience says the answer out loud or tries to help the participant, the judge will inform the moderator and 10 points will be deducted from the team's score.

EXAMPLES:

1. **Claudia is an elderly lady. She has been ill for many years, but no treatments from the doctor have healed her. In her despair, she has begun to seek God.**

   Bible Verses:

   a) *"Jesus turned and saw her. 'Take heart, daughter,' he said, 'your faith has healed you.' And the woman was healed at that moment."* (Matthew 9:22)

   b) *"For whoever does the will of my Father in heaven is my brother and sister and mother."* (Matthew 12:50)

2. **Louis is a very abusive child. He is constantly annoying his classmates, and the teacher has had to talk to his parents and make them see that everyone in the classroom is upset.**

   Bible Verses:

   a) *"He will put the sheep on his right and the goats on his left."* (Matthew 25:33)

   b) *"And if anyone wants to sue you and take your shirt, hand over your coat as well."* (Matthew 5:40)

FOLLOWING THE FOOTPRINTS

SCORE	TIME	PARTICIPANTS	MODE
60 Points Possible (5 per correct answer)	30 seconds to give your answer	1 per team	One team at a time

Items needed:

- The moderator will prepare a questionnaire with 12 different questions for each team and put it in a sealed numbered envelope,
- 12 FOOTPRINTS made of any material
- 2 signs, one that says "START," the other "FINISH,"
- a different colored card for each team.

All teams will choose an envelope from the moderator and then line up at the START in front of the giant footprints on the floor. The moderator will receive the envelope from team #1 and ask a question from the questions inside to the participant from team #1. The participant has 30 seconds to give the answer. If in 30 seconds she correctly answers the question, the she puts her color card on the first footprint. If she doesn't give the correct answer or remains silent, the moderator will say the correct answer out loud and she won't be able to advance. Then the moderator will receive the envelope from the second team and ask that team's participant the first question from that list, and so forth through the teams. Once all teams have been asked question 1, the moderator begins again with team #1 by asking their question #2 and so forth. When a team answers correctly, they advance their colored card marker along the footprints. When a team answers incorrectly, they don't move their colored card marker. The game is over after 12 questions have been asked to each participant. Teams that answer all 12 questions correctly will reach footprint #12 and each receive 60 points. All other teams will receive 5 points for each correct answer they gave.

FOUL: If someone from the audience says the answer aloud, 10 points will be deducted from the team that committed this infraction.

Example:

Rebecca of the "Fishermen" team (red) answered 9 questions for a total of 45 points.

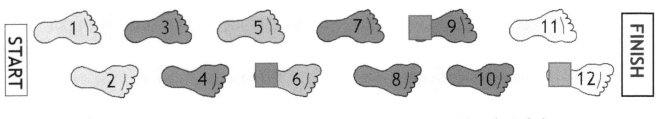

Oliver of the "Matthew" team (blue) answered 6 questions for a total of 30 points.

Cherika of the "Disciples" team (green) answered 12 questions for a total of 60 points.

WHAT IT TEACHES US

SCORE	TIME	PARTICIPANTS	MODE
20 points	1 minute per answer	1 per team	One team at a time

The moderator will prepare a Bible verse corresponding to the Bible verses being studied, as well as a list of 3 VALUES, on a letter-sized sheet of paper for each team. These will be different for each team. The verse and values for each team will be sealed in an envelope with a participation number on the outside.

Each team will pick an envelope. Starting with the envelope from Team #1, the moderator will read aloud the verse and the 3 VALUES. The participant has one minute to state which value relates to the verse, and their rational for choosing that value. If the participant chooses the correct VALUE that goes with the verse, and give the correct rational, the team will receive 20 points. If the participant chooses the right verse but the explanation is incorrect, the judge will give 10 points to the team.

FOUL: Consultation is not allowed. If the participant consults with anyone about the answer, or if someone in the audience gives the correct answer, the judge will note it and will deduct 10 points from the team that committed the infraction.

NOTE: Only one value must be related to the verse while the other 2 will not. The verses should not have the actual value written in it. Remember, this category is reflection.

WHAT ARE VALUES? Values are principles that guide our life (behavior).

LIST OF VALUES: Generosity, respect, gratitude, friendship, responsibility, peace, solidarity, tolerance, honesty, justice, freedom, strength, loyalty, integrity, forgiveness, kindness, humility, perseverance, love, unity, trust.

"Jesus answered, 'If you want to be perfect, go, sell your possessions and give to the poor, and you will have treasure in heaven. Then come, follow me.'" (Matthew 19:21)

| GENEROSITY | RESPECT | LOYALTY |

"You have heard that it was said, 'Eye for eye, and tooth for tooth.' But I tell you, do not resist an evil person. If anyone slaps you on the right cheek, turn to them the other cheek also." (Matthew 5:38-39)

| GRATITUDE | FREEDOM | LOVE |

"For where two or three gather in my name, there am I with them." (Matthew 18:20)

| JUSTICE | INTEGRITY | UNITY |

"… and teaching them to obey everything I have commanded you. And surely I am with you always, to the very end of the age." (Matthew 28:20)

| KINDNESS | PERSEVERANCE | FORGIVENESS |

CHEST OF MEMORIES

SCORE	TIME	PARTICIPANTS	MODE
20 points (10 points per participant)	2 minutes (1 minute per participant)	2 per team	One team at a time

Items Needed:
- Objects of any material
- A wooden chest or trunk, or one made out of cardboard
- Participation numbers

The moderator will place the objects inside the chest/trunk/box beforehand.

Each team will choose a participation number.

Starting with team 1, the moderator will invite the first participant to put his hand into the chest and take out an object without looking. The participant then will have 2 minutes to explain what that object represents from the Bible verses being studied.

If the participant relates his story well, the judge will give him 10 points, and then continue on to the second participant of the same team. The same directions apply to the second participants, as well as to additional teams. Each participant can earn 10 points, for a maximum of 20 points per team.

Note: An object that has been taken out of the chest is not put back in after the participant is finished with it.

FOUL: If a participant consults with his partner or the public, the judge will deduct 10 points from the team.

Examples of objects you could put in the chest:

Star	2:2-10 24:29
Honey	3:4
Bread	4:3, 6:11, 7:9
Fish	13:47, 14:17
Net	4:20-21
Boat	4:21-22, 8:23
tree	21:18-21, 24:32
Crown	27:29

Wheat	3:12, 13:24,
Seed	13:4-38
Linen cloth	27:59
Glass	10:42, 20:22, 26:7
Heart	5:8, 12:34, 22:37
Lamp	Cap. 25
Cross	10:38, 16:24, 27:32-42
Sheep	7:15, 9:36, 10:16, 18:12

MAILBOX

SCORE	TIME	PARTICIPANTS	MODE
20 points	1 minute after the lecture	All the team	One team at a time

Items needed:

- The moderator will prepare a letter written to a Bible character, giving characteristics and hints of who that person is in the letter. He will then put the letter in an envelope. He will prepare a different letter for each team.
- A mailbox of any material in which the moderator will put the envelopes.

The moderator will give participation numbers to the teams using which every manner he chooses.

The moderator will instruct a team participant to put their hand in the mailbox to get a letter to read. The moderator will then read the letter. When the reading is finished, the team has one minute to discuss the letter. At the end of the time, one of the team members must announce to the moderator which person in the Bible the letter is addressed to. If the answer is correct, the judge will give 20 points to the team.

FOUL: If any participant from any of the teams or anyone in the audience speaks during the team's response, the judge will inform the moderator, who will then deduct 10 points from the team that committed the infraction.

EXAMPLES:
I write to you because I know that soon you will walk through the desert of Judea and the Jordan River. They told me that you will be talking about repentance, and that you studied the prophet Isaiah. I know that Jesus will look for you, and I send you this letter so that you are prepared. He will want you to baptize him.
Answer: John the Baptist (chapter 3)

Good evening, I am writing to tell you that the chief priests are trying to catch Jesus. They may offer you thirty pieces of silver. I hope that you receive my letter in time and that you don't accept the pieces of silver, because you will surely regret it and the consequences could be fatal.
Answer: Judas (26:14-16; 27 3-10)

I am sending you this letter because you are an important man. Your daughter has been very sick and it is possible that she has died. But I know that Jesus will be near your house soon, so have courage. I am sure he will do a miracle in your house!
Answer: Jairus (9:18-26)

ORDER OF EVENTS

SCORE	TIME	PARTICIPANTS	MODE
50 points (40 for correct order and 10 for telling the story)	4 minutes (2 to put in order and 2 to tell the story)	1 per team	Simultaneous for putting in order and one at a time to tell the story.

The moderator will put five scenes of a story into a sealed envelope with a participation number on the outside. He will prepare as many stories as there are teams to participate. The story must be different for each team.

When the moderator gives the start signal, each participant will have 2 minutes to put their story scenes into the correct order according to how the biblical event happened. At the end of the time (2 minutes), the moderator will give each participant 2 minutes to tell the story, going in order of the participation number on the outside of their envelopes.

40 points will be given for putting the story scenes into the correct order, and 10 points for telling the story correctly, for a maximum total of 50 points per team.

NOTE: It is best to have the story scenes on 5 separate pieces of paper or cards so that the participants can move them around to put them into the correct order instead of just having all of the scenes on the same piece of paper.

FOUL: Consultation with the coach or anyone else is prohibited, and will result in disqualification of the team for this game.

Example: Jesus' Crucifixion (Numbers are printed here only to show the correct order of the pictures.)

CRAFTS CATEGORY

ANSWER AND DRAW

SCORE	TIME	PARTICIPANTS	MODE
30 points	6 minutes – 1 minute per participant to answer and draw, 1 minute explanation.	5 per team	One team at a time

Items needed:
- The moderator will present a base drawing, such as a prison, city, mountains, sea, etc., on a sheet of paper for each team to draw on. The drawing must be different for each team.
- Colored markers for the team drawing.

The moderator will give each team an envelope containing the base drawing, as well as a theme story and 5 different questions for each team about that story. The envelopes will be numbered on the outside.

When it is time for the first team to start, the team will hand the envelope to the moderator, who will tape the base picture to a board or wall that the team can easily reach to draw on.

The team will form a line in front of the base drawing with the 5 participants. The moderator will announce their theme story, and then ask the first participant a question from the envelope. When the moderator finishes the first question, the time is started of 1 minute per participant. If the participant answers the question correctly, he will start drawing on the base picture, illustrating the theme story that they have been given. He draws until his minute is up. If the participant answers incorrectly, he does not proceed to draw on the picture, his turn is over, and the moderator continues by asking the next participant of the team a question. If that participant answers the question correctly, he goes and continues the same drawing that the first person started, and so forth. After all 5 participants of the team have had the opportunity to answer a question and draw, the moderator will ask a team representative to explain the picture they drew (1 minute time limit).

After the first team finishes, the moderator moves on to the second team, and so forth.

THE JUDGES AWARD POINTS BASED ON THESE CRITERIA:
Clarity of the drawing: 5-10 points
Drawing is relevant to the subject of study: 5-10 points
The picture is drawn realistically (proportionate sizes, etc.): 5-10 points

Examples (Questions can be found in the back of this book):

- **The Baptism of Jesus 3:13-17**

    - What happened to the heavens when Jesus was baptized? A. They were opened. (3:16)
    - Who did Jesus see descend as a dove upon him? A. The Spirit of God (3:16 25).
    - What did the voice that came from heaven say? A. This is my beloved son, in whom I am pleased 3:17)
    - Who baptized in water for repentance? A. John the Baptist (3:11)
    - Who came from Galilee for John to baptize? A. Jesus (3:13)

- **The Parable of the Sower 13:1-9**

    - The kingdom of heaven is like what? A. Like a man who sowed good seed in his field. (13:24)
    - What was the explanation for the seed that fell on the road? A. When someone hears the word of the kingdom and does not understand it, the evil one comes and snatches what was sown in his heart. (13:19)
    - Explain about the seed that fell on the rocky soil. A. This is the one who hears the word, and immediately receives it with joy, but is of short duration because when affliction or persecution comes because of the word, then he stumbles. (13:21)
    - What was Jesus' explanation of the seed that fell on thorns? A. This is the one who hears the word, but the eagerness of this age and the deceitfulness of riches choke the word, and it becomes unfruitful. (13:22)
    - What is the explanation that Jesus gave about the seed that fell on good ground? A. This is the one who produces a crop, yielding a hundred, sixty or thirty times what was sown. (13:23)

- **The Parable of the Wandering Sheep 18:10-14**

- **Jesus Anointed at Bethany 26:6-13**

- **Peter Disowns Jesus 26:69-75**

- **The Crucifixion of Jesus 27:32-50**

- **Jesus Has Risen 28:1-11**

DRAW IT

SCORE	TIME	PARTICIPANTS	MODE
30 points total	3 minutes	2 per team	One team at a time

Note: This game is similar to the popular game Pictionary.

Items needed:

- The moderator will prepare a list of themes (Bible events and characters) from the Bible passages being studied. Two themes, on separate pieces of paper) will be placed into sealed envelopes with a participation number on the outside for each team.
- A large sheet of paper or a blackboard/whiteboard
- Markers or chalk

The moderator will give a sealed envelope containing two themes to each team. When the game begins, the moderator will receive the envelope from team #1 and will give one of the themes to one of the participants. That participant will have 1 minute to draw the theme while their teammate tries to figure out what he/she is drawing. If the teammate guesses the theme within the 1 minute time limit, their team receives 15 points. Then the roles are reversed. The guesser now becomes the drawer and receives the other theme from the moderator, and the one who drew first becomes the guesser. Again the time limit is 1 minute, and 15 points goes to the team for a correct answer within the time limit.

The same procedure is followed with the following teams until all teams have finished.

FOUL: If the audience or other team members interrupts by giving any response, the team's participation in that round is canceled and no points are awarded.

- **The Magi Visit the Messiah 2:1-12**

- **The Baptism of Jesus 3:13-17**

- **The Calling of Matthew 9:9-13**

- **Man with a Shriveled Hand 12:9-14**

- **The Parable of the Sower 13:1-9**

- **Jesus Feeds the Five Thousand 14:1-12**

- **Jesus Comes to Jerusalem as King 21:1-11**

COLLAGE

SCORE	TIME	PARTICIPANTS	MODE
40 points	6 minutes (5 to make the collage and 1 to explain it)	3 per team	Simultaneous to do it, and one team at a time to explain it.

Items needed:

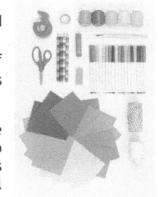

- The moderator will prepare **1 theme for each team** in sealed envelopes, with the participation number on the outside.
- Cardboard or letter-sized paper, scissors, white glue, paper of different colors and textures, such as tissue paper, newspaper, gloss etc.

The moderator will start the game with a whistle – all teams will participate at the same time. Each team will have 5 minutes to make a collage to illustrate the theme that they received in their envelope. Team members may talk with one another, but not with anyone else. After 5 minutes, all teams will stop working on their collages. Each team will appoint a representative from among the three who will have 1 minute to explain their collage.

THE JUDGES WILL AWARD POINTS BASED ON THE FOLLOWING CRITERIA:
Relevance to the theme: 5-10 points
Creativity and good use of colors: 5-10 points
Use of materials: 5-10 points
Explanation: 5-10 points

FOUL: 5 points will be deducted from the team that is talking to each other during the explanation of the collages by any of the participating teams.

Examples:

- **The Magi Visit the Messiah 2:1-12**

- **The Baptism of Jesus 3:13-17**

- **The Calling of Matthew 9:9-13**

- **Man with a Shriveled Hand 12:9-14**

- **The Parable of the Sower 13:1-9**

- **Jesus Feeds the Five Thousand 14:1-12**

- **Jesus Comes to Jerusalem as King 21:1-11**

PUPPETS

SCORE	TIME	PARTICIPANTS	MODE
30 points	5 minutes	2 per team	Simultaneous make the puppets and one team at a time will explain.

Items needed:

- The moderator will prepare an envelope for each team with the name of the Bible character the team needs to portray and a participation number on the outside. This Bible character must be different for each team.
- Paper bag, white glue, paper of different textures and colors wool or yarn, markers, scissors for each team.

The moderator will ask the two participants of each team to sit on the floor or on a table, along with their envelop and supplies.

When the moderator blows his whistle, each team will create a puppet that represents their Bible character. At the end of 5 minutes, all the teams must stop working. Then in order of participation number, 1 member from each team will have 1 minute to use their puppet to explain who they are.

THE JUDGES WILL AWARD POINTS BASED ON THE FOLLOW CRITERIA:

Creativity and workmanship of the puppet: 5-10 points

Explanation: 5-10 points

Good use of the materials: 5-10 points

FOUL: 5 points are deducted from teams that talk during the explanation of their character or while other teams are presenting.

NOTE: At the end of the activity, an exhibition can be made to appreciate the work the children did and to reward their creativity.

CHARACTERS:

- **Jesus**
- **John the Baptist**
- **Matthew**
- **Peter**
- **Judas**
- **Pilate**
- **Canaanite woman**
- **Simon of Cyrene**
- **Mary Magdalene**
- **Joseph from Arimathea**

FLAGS

SCORE	TIME	PARTICIPANTS	MODE
30 points possible	5 minutes for creating the flag, 1 for explanation	2 per team	Simultaneous to make the flags and one team at a time to explain

Items needed:

- The moderator will prepare 1 card per team, on which is written the name of a place or Bible character from the biblical passages being studied. Each card must be different. These cards are placed in sealed envelopes with a participation number on the outside.

- Sheets of paper, colored paper, wooden or plastic sticks of 60 cm. White glue, scissors, markers.

Each team will receive an envelope and materials to create their flag. When the moderator gives the signal, each team will have 5 minutes to create a flag that somehow illustrates the place or character that they received in their envelope. At the end of 5 minutes, all teams will stop working. Then one participant from each team will have 1 minute to explain their flag. This will be done according to their participation number.

THE JUDGES WILL AWARD POINTS BASED ON THE FOLLOWING CRITERIA:
Quality of workmanship and creativity of the flag: 5-10 points

Explanation: 5-10 points

Good use of the materials: 5-10 points

FOUL: If during the explanation, a different participant or a member of the audience speaks, 10 points will be deducted from the team that commits this infraction.

THEMES:
- The desert, 3: 1-3, 4: 1, 11: 7, 14:15, 15:33
- The Jordan River, 3: 5, 6, 13; 4:15, 25; 19: 1
- The Sea of Galilee, 4: 15,18, 15:29
- Bethany, 21:17; 26: 6
- Gethsemane, 26:36
- Golgotha, 27:33

ACTION CATEGORY

CHARADES

SCORE	TIME	PARTICIPANTS	MODE
25 points	2 minutes	5 per team	One team at a time

The moderator will write down a theme/Bible story on note cards, a different one per team, and put them in sealed envelopes with participation numbers on the outside. The envelopes must not be opened until it is time for the team to participate.

The participant who chooses the envelope must act out the theme/Bible story so that his 4 remaining teammates can try to guess the theme/Bible story he is trying to communicate through his actions. The team has 2 minutes to give the correct answer.

The judge awards 25 POINTS if the team answers correctly. If the team answers incorrectly, the judge indicates it and no score is given to that team. The moderator should say the correct answer out loud if it is not guessed.

FOUL: If an audience member interrupts, the judge will disqualify the team from the game and no points will be given.

Possible themes/stories:

- **The Magi Visit the Messiah 2:1-12**
- **The Baptism of Jesus 3:13-17**
- **The Calling of Matthew 9:9-13**
- **Man with a Shriveled Hand 12:9-14**
- **The Parable of the Sower 13:1-9**
- **Jesus Feeds the Five Thousand 14:1-12**
- **Jesus Comes to Jerusalem as King 21:1-11**

POETRY

SCORE	TIME	PARTICIPANTS	MODE
50 points maximum	1 minute	2 per team	One team at a time

Each team will receive a participation number.

The moderator starts with the first team to participate, giving them one minute for the 2 of participants to present the poem together.

THE JUDGES WILL AWARD POINTS BASED ON THE FOLLOWING CRITERIA:

Gestures: 5-10 points

Coordination between the 2 participants: 5-10 points

Intonation: 5-10 points

The poem must be prepared by the team:

Having unpublished lyrics: 5-10 points

Theme is related to the passages that are being studied: 5-10 points

Note: The poem must have 3 stanzas and the presentation must be no longer than 1 minute.

EXAMPLE:
I raise my eyes and see from afar
A man coming out of the desert
He seems tired, full of sand
But his face is of victory

Turn the stones into loaves,
All these cities I will give you
The enemy offered him, but he did not give up
Each time with a word from God he answered him.

It's Jesus my savior
Forty days and forty nights fasted
He overcame temptation and the angels served him
Behold, know Jesus my savior.

ACROSTIC (NEW GAME)

SCORE	TIME	PARTICIPANTS	MODE
40 points	5 minutes	2 per team	Simultaneously each team creates and then one team at a time presents.

The moderator will prepare cards (enough for each team) on which is written a name of a Bible character that has been studied (a different name for each team). The card, along with a blank card, will be placed in a sealed envelope with a participation number on the outside.

Each team will receive an envelope. All teams will participate at the same time.

When the moderator gives the start signal, all teams will start at the same time and will have 5 minutes to make an acrostic using the name they received in their envelope (see example below).

At the end of the 5 minutes, each team must stop work. Then the moderator will give one participant from each team, 1 minute to present their acrostic (in participation number order).

THE JUDGES WILL AWARD POINTS BASED ON THE FOLLOWING CRITERIA:

Creativity: 5-10 points

Intonation: 5-10 points

Creativity of presentation: 5-10 points

Acrostic related to the theme: 5-10 points

CHARACTERS:
- Jesus
- Matthew
- Peter
- Judas
- Pilate
- Andrew
- James
- Philip
- Thomas

EXAMPLE:

J ewels the savior has given me
E ntirely his life he gave
S orry for failing
U nited to you I always want to be
S ilence I will keep when you want to talk to me

DRAMA

SCORE	TIME	PARTICIPANTS	MODE
50 points	5 minutes	All the team and coaches	One team at a time

The moderator will write down a biblical event on cards, a different one for each team, and then place them in sealed envelopes with participation numbers on the outside.

With all teams starting at the same time, the moderator will give the go ahead, and the teams will have 5 minutes to prepare their dramas with the themes that they received in their envelopes. The drama should be presented as if it were happening today in modern times.

After the 5 minutes of preparation time, coaches must leave and the teams must present their dramas in the order of their participation numbers.

Once team #1 has finished, team #2 will begin, etc...

Note: It's important to take into account that teams must bring their costumes, decorations and other props they wish to use with them to the game.

THE JUDGES WILL AWARD POINTS BASED ON THE FOLLOWING CRITERIA:

Participation of the whole team: 5-10 points

The ability to represent the story accurately: 5-10 points

The fluidity of the dialogue: 5-10 points

The use of available resources (props, decorations, etc.): 5-10 points

The drama is faithful to the teaching of the event/theme: 5-10 points

FOUL: 10 points will be deducted from a team if they speak during another team's presentation.

Possible Biblical Events:
- **The Magi Visit the Messiah 2:1-12**
- **The Baptism of Jesus 3:13-17**
- **The Calling of Matthew 9:9-13**
- **Man with a Shriveled Hand 12:9-14**
- **The Parable of the Sower 13:1-9**
- **Jesus Feeds the Five Thousand 14:1-12**
- **Jesus Comes to Jerusalem as King 21:1-11**

BREAKING NEWS

SCORE	TIME	PARTICIPANTS	MODE
20 points possible per team	4 minutes (3 to prepare and 2 to give the news)	4 per team	One team at a time

Items needed:

- The moderator will put a biblical event or bible passage on note cards, a different one for each team, and then place them in sealed envelopes with participation numbers on the outside.
- Letter size piece of paper and pencil or pen for each team.

Each team will choose an envelope. When the moderator gives the go ahead, the first team will have 3 minutes to prepare their news report about the event they received in their envelope.

After the 3 minutes of preparation time, one of the team participants will present the news report as informatively, creatively and interestingly as possible.

Once team #1 has finished, team #2 will begin.

THE JUDGES WILL AWARD POINTS BASED ON THE FOLLOWING CRITERIA:

Creativity: 5-10 points
Fluidity of the dialogue: 5-10 points

Possible Topics:

- **Jesus Is Tested in the Wilderness 4:1-11**
- **Jesus Is Tested in the Wilderness 8:5-13**
- **Jesus Heals Many 8:14-17**
- **Jesus Calms the Storm 8:23-27**
- **Jesus Forgives and Heals a Paralyzed Man 9:1-8**
- **Jesus Raises a Dead Girl and Heals a Sick Woman 9:18-26**
- **Jesus Heals the Blind and the Mute 9:27-34**
- **Jesus Feeds the Five Thousand 14:13-21**
- **Judas Hangs Himself 27:1-10**

MUSIC CATEGORY

NEW SONG

SCORE	TIME	PARTICIPANTS	MODE
50 points	3 minutes	All the team	One team at a time

Each team must present an unpublished song, which will be sung by the whole team. The team can present it with choreography or spiritual dancing, etc. The song must have:

1. Unpublished lyrics (lyrics must be written by the team)
2. Lyrics related to the theme of Bible Quizzing.
3. The actual tune may be from a published Christian song, but the lyrics must be changed.
4. Minumum of two verses, maximum of four.
5. Maximum duration of three minutes.

THE JUDGES WILL AWARD POINTS BASED ON THE FOLLOWING CRITERIA:

Quality of the Unpublished lyrics: 5-10 points

Lyrics related to the theme of the Bible Quizzing Study: 5-10 points

Music (intonation, harmony): 5-10 points

Creativity in the presentation: 5-10 points

Full team participation: 5-10 points

The song can be presented in each competition to improve this category.

SINGING THE TEXT

SCORE	TIME	PARTICIPANTS	MODE
20 points	3 minutes	All the team	One team at a time

The moderator will prepare cards with Bible verses (a different one for each team) and put them in sealed envelopes with participation numbers on the outside.

When the moderator gives the start signal for the first team to start, the team will have 3 minutes to read the verse and then come up with a tune and movements. The team will then present the "song."

THE JUDGES WILL AWARD POINTS BASED ON THE FOLLOWING CRITERIA:

Intonation and harmony: 5-10 points

Creativity in the presentation: 5-10 points

FOUL: If a team talks while another team is presenting, the judge will call attention to it and 10 points will be deducted from the team that commits this infraction.

MEMORY VERSES

"The virgin will conceive and give birth to a son, and they will call him Immanuel" (which means "God with us")	1:23
As soon as Jesus was baptized, he went up out of the water. At that moment heaven was opened, and he saw the Spirit of God descending like a dove and alighting on him.	3:16
Jesus answered, "It is written: 'Man shall not live on bread alone, but on every word that comes from the mouth of God.	4:4
From that time on Jesus began to preach, "Repent, for the kingdom of heaven has come near."	4:17
Blessed are the pure in heart, for they will see God.	5:8
You are the light of the world. A town built on a hill cannot be hidden.	5:14
But seek first his kingdom and his righteousness, and all these things will be given to you as well.	6:33
But small is the gate and narrow the road that leads to life, and only a few find it.	7:14
Every tree that does not bear good fruit is cut down and thrown into the fire. [20] Thus, by their fruit you will recognize them.	7:19-20
Then he said to his disciples, "The harvest is plentiful but the workers are few. [38] Ask the Lord of the harvest, therefore, to send out workers into his harvest field	9:37-38
Whoever finds their life will lose it, and whoever loses their life for my sake will find it.	10:39
Come to me, all you who are weary and burdened, and I will give you rest.	11:28
A good man brings good things out of the good stored up in him, and an evil man brings evil things out of the evil stored up in him.	12:35
… and begged him to let the sick just touch the edge of his cloak, and all who touched it were healed.	14:36
But the things that come out of a person's mouth come from the heart, and these defile them.	15:18
Simon Peter answered, "You are the Messiah, the Son of the living God.	16:16
Then Jesus said to his disciples, "Whoever wants to be my disciple must deny themselves and take up their cross and follow me."	16:24

And he said: "Truly I tell you, unless you change and become like little children, you will never enter the kingdom of heaven."	18:3
Jesus looked at them and said, "With man this is impossible, but with God all things are possible."	19:26
just as the Son of Man did not come to be served, but to serve, and to give his life as a ransom for many.	20:28
The crowds that went ahead of him and those that followed shouted, "Hosanna to the Son of David!" "Blessed is he who comes in the name of the Lord!" "Hosanna in the highest heaven!"	21:9
Jesus replied: "'Love the Lord your God with all your heart and with all your soul and with all your mind."	22:37
Because of the increase of wickedness, the love of most will grow cold, but the one who stands firm to the end will be saved.	24:12-13
Therefore keep watch, because you do not know the day or the hour.	25:13
Going a little farther, he fell with his face to the ground and prayed, "My Father, if it is possible, may this cup be taken from me. Yet not as I will, but as you will."	26:39
The angel said to the women, "Do not be afraid, for I know that you are looking for Jesus, who was crucified. He is not here; he has risen, just as he said. Come and see the place where he lay."	28:5-6
Therefore go and make disciples of all nations, baptizing them in the name of the Father and of the Son and of the Holy Spirit, [20] and teaching them to obey everything I have commanded you. And surely I am with you always, to the very end of the age.	28:19-20

QUESTIONS

CHAPTER 1

1. Whose descendant was Jesus?
   A. Abraham (son of David, son of Abraham) 1:1
2. Who did Abraham father?
   A. Isaac 1:2-3
3. Who was Isaac's father?
   A. Abraham
4. Whom did Isaac father?
   A. Jacob 1:2
5. Who did Jacob father?
   A. Judah and his brothers 1:2
6. How many generations were there from Abraham to David, from David until the deportation to Babylon, and from Babylon to Christ?
   A. 14 generations. 1:17
7. How the Jesus' birth come about?
   A. His mother Mary was pledged to be married to Joseph, but before they came together, she was found to be pregnant through the Holy Spirit. 1:18
8. What was the name of the husband of Mary, mother of Jesus?
   A. Joseph 1:18
9. What does the name "Jesus" mean?
   A. Savior 1:21
10. What does "Immanuel" mean?
    A. God with us 1:23

CHAPTER 2

11. Where was Jesus born?
    A. In Bethlehem of Judea 2:1
12. Who was King when Jesus was born?
    A. Herod 2:1
13. Who came from the East?
    A. Magi 2:1
14. What gifts did the Magi offer the child?
    A. Gold, frankincense and myrrh 2:11

CHAPTER 3

15. Who was preaching in the desert of Judea?
    A. John the Baptist 3:1
16. What did John the Baptist preach in the desert of Judea?
    A. Repent because the kingdom of heaven has come near. 3:2
17. Who ate locusts and wild honey?
    A. John the Baptist 3:4
18. What did John the Baptist wear and have around his waist?
    A. Camel hair clothes and a leather belt 3:4
19. According to John the Baptist, what happens to every tree that does not bear good fruit?
    A. It is cut down and thrown into the fire 3:10

20. Who came from Galilee to be baptized by John?
    A. Jesus 3:13
21. What happened to the heavens when Jesus was baptized?
    A. They were opened 3:16
22. Who did Jesus see descend as a dove and come upon him?
    A. The Spirit of God 3:16
23. What did the voice that came from heaven say?
    A. "This is my Son, whom I love; with him I am well pleased." 3:17

CHAPTER 4

24. Why was Jesus led by the Spirit into the desert?
    A. To be tempted by the devil 4:1
25. How long did Jesus fast in the desert?
    A. 40 days and 40 nights 4:2
26. What did Jesus say to Peter and Andrew?
    A. "Come, follow me, and I will send you out to fish for people." 4:19
27. What job did Peter and Andrew have?
    A. They were fishermen 4:18
28. After Peter and Andrew followed Jesus, Jesus found two other brothers. Who were they?
    A. James and John 4:21
29. What were James, John and their Father Zebedee doing?
    A. Preparing their nets 4:21

CHAPTER 5

30. When Jesus went up the mountain, who came to him?
    A. His disciples 5:1
31. According to the Sermon on the Mount, to whom does the kingdom of heaven belong?
    A. To the poor in spirit 5:3
32. In Matthew 5:4, what is the promise for those who mourn?
    A. they will be comforted 5:4
33. Who will receive the earth as an inheritance?
    A. The meek 5:5

CHAPTER 6

34. Where does Jesus tell us to pray?
    A. In our room. 6:6
35. When we pray, what should we not do?
    A. Do not keep on babbling like pagans. 6:7
36. Who knows what needs we have before we ask for it?
    A. Your Father who is in heaven. 6:8

CHAPTER 7

37. Complete the phrase in verse 7:7, "Ask and it ....
    A. will be given to you; seek and you will find; knock and the door will be opened to you." 7:7
38. Who will give good things to those who ask for it?
    A. Our Father who is in heaven 7:11
39. What do all good trees bear?
    A. Good fruit (7:17)
40. In what way does Jesus teach?
    A. With authority 7:29

CHAPTER 8

41. What happened when Jesus entered the boat?
    A. His disciples followed him. 8:23
42. What arose in the sea when Jesus was sleeping?
    A. A furious storm 8:24
43. When Jesus was awakened, what did his disciples tell him?
    A. "Lord, save us! We're going to drown!" 8:25
44. What was Jesus' response when he was awakened?
    A. "You of little faith, why are you so afraid?" 8:26
45. To whom did Jesus say, "You of little faith?
    A. To his disciples 8:26

CHAPTER 9

46. What did the synagogue leader say when he came and knelt before Jesus?
    A. "My daughter has just died. But come and put your hand on her, and she will live." 9:18
47. What did the woman who touched the edge of Jesus' cloak say to herself?
    A. "If I only touch his cloak, I will be healed." 9:19
48. For how many years did the woman feel sick before touching the edge of Jesus' cloak?
    A. 12 Years 9:20
49. What did Jesus say when the woman touched him?
    A. "Your faith has healed you." 9:22
50. When Jesus entered the house of the synagogue leader, there was a great commotion. What did Jesus say?
    A. "Go away. The girl is not dead but asleep." 9:24

CHAPTER 10

51. Who would speak for the disciples when they were brought before governors and kings?
    A. The Spirit of your Father (God) 10:18-19
52. Why would Jesus' disciples be hated?
    A. Because of Jesus 10:22
53. What will the Lord do with those who acknowledge Him before men?
    A. He will acknowledge them before his Father who is in heaven. 10:32
54. Who will the Lord deny before his Father who is in heaven?
    A. Those who deny him in front of men. 10:33
55. What did Jesus say about those who love father or mother more than him?
    A. They are not worthy of him. 10:38
56. What must we do to be worthy of him?
    A. Take up our cross and follow him. 10:38

CHAPTER 11

57. Where was John the Baptist while Jesus taught and preached in the towns of Galilee?
    A. In prison. 11:1
58. What did John the Baptist do when he heard about the deeds of the Messiah?
    A. He sent his disciples to Jesus. 11:2
59. What did John the Baptist's disciples ask Jesus?
    A. "Are you the one who is to come, or should we expect someone else?" 11:3
60. What did Jesus say to the disciples who John the Baptist sent?
    A. Go back and report to John what you hear and see. 11:4
61. To whom is the good news proclaimed?
    A. To the poor 11:5

62. Who said, "Blessed is anyone who does not stumble on account of me."?
    A. Jesus 11:6

CHAPTER 12

63. Jesus and his disciples walked through some grain fields on the Sabbath. What did they feel?
    A. Hunger 12:1
64. What did the disciples do when they were hungry?
    A. The picked some heads of grain and ate them. 12:2
65. What did the Pharisees tell Jesus when they saw the disciples picking grain and eating on the Sabbath?
    A. "Look! Your disciples are doing what is unlawful on the Sabbath." 12:2
66. Who were the only ones who could eat the consecrated bread?
    A. The priests 12:4
67. Who is Lord of the Sabbath?
    A. The Son of Man (Jesus) 12:8

CHAPTER 13

68. The kingdom of heaven is like what?
    A. Like a man who sowed good seed in his field. 13:24
69. Who came, and what did he do, while the men slept?
    A. His enemy came and sowed weeds among the wheat. 13:25
70. What appeared when the wheat sprouted and formed heads?
    A. Weeds 13:26
71. What did the owner say to his servants about the weeds that had grown up next to the wheat?
    A. An enemy has done this. 13:28
72. How did the owner respond to the servants who wanted to pull up the weeds?
    A. "'No, because while you are pulling the weeds, you may uproot the wheat with them. Let both grow together until the harvest." 13:29-30

CHAPTER 14

73. Where did Jesus go when he heard about the death of John the Baptist?
    A. **He withdrew by boat privately to a solitary place.** 14:13
74. The people followed Jesus on foot from the cities, and when Jesus saw the crowd that had followed him, what did he feel, and what did he do for them?
    A. He had compassion on them, and Jesus healed those who were sick. 14:14
75. What did Jesus reply when the disciples told him, "Send the crowds away, so they can go to the villages and buy themselves some food."?
    A. "They do not need to go away. You give them something to eat." 14:16
76. What did the disciples have to feed the crowd?
    A. Five loaves of bread and two fish.14:17
77. What did Jesus do with the five loaves of bread and two fish?
    A. Taking the five loaves and the two fish and looking up to heaven, he gave thanks and broke the loaves. Then he gave them to the disciples, and the disciples gave them to the people. 14:19
78. When the had eaten and were full, what did the disciples do?
    A. They picked up twelve basketfuls of pieces that were left over. 14:20
79. How many men ate, without counting women and children?
    A.: Five thousand men 14:21

CHAPTER 15

80. To what region did Jesus go after talking about what contaminates people?
    A. To the region of Tyre and Sidon 15:21

81. What problem did the Canaanite woman have who cried out to the Lord?
    A. Her daughter was demon-possessed and suffering terribly. 15:22

82. What did Jesus do in response to the cry of the Canaanite woman?
    A. He did not answer a word. 15:23

83. What did the disciples urge Jesus to do?
    A. "Send her away, for she keeps crying out after us."15:23

84. To whom was Jesus sent?
    A. Only to the lost sheep of Israel. 15:24

85. What did the Canaanite woman say to Jesus?
    A. Lord, help me! 15:25

CHAPTER 16-17

86. How will the Son of Man reward each person?
    A. According to what they have done. 16:27

87. Where were Jesus and his disciples when Jesus said, "The Son of Man is going to be delivered into the hands of men"?
    A. In Galilee 17:22

88. On what day was Jesus going to raised?
    A. The third day 17:23

89. What did his disciples feel when they heard that Jesus was going to die?
    A. They were **filled with grief.**17:23

CHAPTER 18

90. Complete the text: And he said: "Truly I tell you, unless you change…
    A. and become like little children, you will never enter the kingdom of heaven." 18:2

91. What does a man do who has one hundred sheep and loses one?
    A. He leaves the ninety-nine on the hills and goes to look for the one that wandered off. 18:12

92. What does the man do who finds the sheep that was lost?
    A. He is happier about that one sheep than about the ninety-nine that did not wander off. 18:13

CHAPTER 19

93. Why did people bring their little children to Jesus?
    A. To place his hands on them and pray for them. 19:13

94. What did the disciples do when they saw the children coming to Jesus?
    A. They rebuked them. 19:13

95. What did Jesus say to the disciples when they tried to keep the children away from Jesus?
    A. "Let the little children come to me, and do not hinder them, for the kingdom of heaven belongs to such as these."19:14

CHAPTER 20

96. Where was Jesus going with his disciples when he said to them, "We are going up to Jerusalem, and the Son of Man will be delivered over to the chief priests and the teachers of the law"?
    A. To Jerusalem 20:17

97. Why would Jesus be handed over to the Gentiles and when would he be resurrected?
    A. To be mocked, whipped and crucified and on the third day he will be raised to life! 20:19

CHAPTER 21

98. What did Jesus do with those who were buying and selling in the temple?
   A. He drove them out. 21:12

99. After Jesus had purified the temple, whom did he heal?
   A. The blind and lame. 21:14

100. Who were outraged when they saw the wonderful things that Jesus was doing?
   A. The chief priests and teachers of the law. 21:15

101. After purifying the temple, where did Jesus go?
   A. To Bethany 21:17

CHAPTER 22

102. Who came to Jesus saying that there is no resurrection?
   A. The Sadducees 22:23

103. What did Jesus say we will be like at the resurrection?
   A. Like the angels in heaven. 22:30

104. What did God say about himself in Matthew 22:32?
   A. "I am the God of Abraham, the God of Isaac, and the God of Jacob."

CHAPTER 24

105. What will happen after the "distress of those days"?
   A. "The sun will be darkened, and the moon will not give its light; the stars will fall from the sky, and the heavenly bodies will be shaken.' 24:29

106. What will happen to all the peoples of the earth at the coming of the Son of Man?
   A. They will mourn. 24:30

107. How will all the peoples of the earth see the Son of Man coming from heaven?
   A. On the clouds of heaven, with power and great glory. 24:30

108. Whom will Jesus send to gather his chosen ones at his coming?
   A. His angels. 24:31

109. Did you memorize Matthew 24:35? If so, what is it?
   A. "Heaven and earth will pass away, but my words will never pass away." 24:35

110. Who is the only one who knows the day and time that Jesus will come a second time?
   A. Only the Father (God) 24:36

111. Why should we always be prepared for the second coming of Jesus?
   A. He will come at an hour when you do not expect him. 24:44

CHAPTER 25

112. A man who went on a journey and called his servants and gave them his wealth was compared to what?
   A. To the kingdom of heaven. 25:14

113. How did the man distribute his bags of gold?
   A. To the first servant he gave 5 bags of gold, to the second servant 2 bags of gold, and to the third servant he gave 1 bag of gold. 25:15

114. What did the servant who received 5 bags of gold do, and how much did he earn?
   A. He put it to work and earned another 5 bags of gold. 25:16

CHAPTER 26

115. In whose house was Jesus when he was in Bethany?
   A. In the house of Simon the leper. 26:6

116. A woman came to Jesus while he was at the house of Simon the leper. What did she do to Jesus?
   A. She poured an alabaster jar of expensive perfume on Jesus' head. 26:7

117. Why were the disciples angry when the woman poured the perfume on Jesus?
     A. Because they said it was a waste and could have been sold to help the poor. 26:8-9
118. What did Jesus say the woman who poured the perfume on him had done?
     A. She has done a beautiful thing to me. 26:10
119. Why did the woman pour the perfume on Jesus?
     A. To prepare him for burial. 26:12

CHAPTER 27

120. Who helped carry Jesus' cross?
     A. A man named Simon from Cyrene. 27:32
121. Where was Jesus crucified?
     A. On Golgotha 27.33
122. What does "Golgotha" mean?
     A. The place of the skull. 27:33
123. What was Jesus given to drink on the cross?
     A. Wine mixed with gall. (Gall was possibly a pain killer or poison.) 27:34
124. What was the written charge against Jesus they placed above Jesus' head when they crucified Him?
     A. THIS IS JESUS THE KING OF THE JEWS. 27:37
125. How many thieves were crucified with Jesus?
     A. Two 27:38
126. What happened from noon until 3:00 in the afternoon when Jesus was crucified?
     A. Darkness came over all the land. 27:45

CHAPTER 28

127. Who came to the tomb on the Sabbath?
     A. Mary Magdalene and the other Mary. 28:1
128. Who removed the stone from the tomb?
     A. An Angel of the Lord. 28:2
129. What was the appearance of the angel like who removed the stone from the tomb?
     A. Like lightning and his clothes were white as snow. 28:3
130. In addition to fear and trembling, the guards were like what when they saw the angel?
     A. Like dead men. 28:4
131. What did the angel say to the women who were looking for Jesus in the tomb?
     A. "Do not be afraid, for I know that you are looking for Jesus, who was crucified. He is not here; he has risen, just as he said." 28:5:6
132. What did the women do when Jesus met them on the road and said, "Greetings!"
     A. They came to him, clasped his feet and worshiped him. 28:9
133. Where did the disciples go after Jesus' resurrection?
     A. To the mountain in Galilee where Jesus had told them to go. 28:16
134. What did the disciples do when they saw the risen Jesus?
     A. They worshiped him. 28:17
135. Finish this verse: Jesus said, "All authority in heaven and on earth …
     A. has been given to me. 28:18
136. In Matthew 28:19-20, Jesus gave his disciples what we call the Great Commission. He told his disciples then and now to, "Go and make ….."
     A. "… disciples of all nations, baptizing them in the name of the Father and of the Son and of the Holy Spirit, and teaching them to obey everything I have commanded you."
137. How long will Jesus be with us?
     A. Always, to the very end of the age. 28:26

Lightning Source UK Ltd.
Milton Keynes UK
UKHW030648171121
394105UK00007B/250

9 781635 800838